Other books by
Carmen & Rosemary Martínez Jover

Purchase at:
www.amazon.com & www.carmenmartinezjover.com

I want to have a child,
Whatever it takes!

Recipes of
how babies are made*

A tiny itsy bitsy gift of life,
an egg donor story: girls*

A tiny itsy bitsy gift of life,
an egg donor story: boys*

The Baby Kangaroo
Treasure Hunt*

Available in:
English, Español, Français, Italiano,
Português, Svenska, Türkiye, Česky, Русский & Nederlands

We dedicate this book
to all those who strive to reach for
the **treasures in their lives.**

Carmen & Rosemary Martinez Jover

Text copyright © 2009 Carmen Martínez Jover
www.carmenmartinezjover.com
Illustrations copyright © 2009 Rosemary Martínez
www.rosemarymartinez.com

ISBN: 978-607-00-6545-3

The Twin Kangaroo Treasure Hunt
1st edition February 2013

Story: Carmen Martínez Jover
Illustrations: Rosemary Martínez
Design support: Victor Nieto, Judith Ferado & Erwin Ritschl

Special thanks to www.ami-ac.com, www.endometriosis.org & www.iwannagetpregnant.com

The Twin Kangaroo Treasure Hunt

Written by
Carmen Martínez Jover

Illustrated by
Rosemary Martínez

There were once
two kangaroos:
Jack and Sam.

They lived very happily
in their cosy little home.

One day, while they were having an ice cream at the fair and watching all the little kangaroos playing around them, Sam said, "Jack, wouldn't it be lovely to have our own twin kangaroos?".

Jack smiled and replied,
"Yes. Let's go and visit Wise William so he can give us some advice."

"Hello, Wise William,"
said Jack and Sam.

"What a lovely surprise to see you!"
replied Wise William,
"What may I do for you?"

"We need your advice. You see...
we want to have our own
twin kangaroos and
we don't know where to start,"
they said.

"Wonderful!
I have just what you need.
Let me see…"
he said, as he searched in
his old treasure trunk.

**The Twin Kangaroo
Treasure Hunt!**

"On this there is a list
of things you need
to have your own twin kangaroos.
Once you discover where
to get them all,
come back and I will tell you
what to do next."

12

Jack and Sam read
the curled scroll containing
The Twin Kangaroo Treasure Hunt
very carefully.

"OK, the first thing we can tick off the list is sperm," said Jack.

"We both have sperm, but it doesn't really matter whose sperm we use, the twins will be both of ours anyway," said Sam.

16

"We can use your sperm or mine or both," said Jack.

"I am so excited soon we will both be Dads," said Sam.

Jack and Sam happily ticked off
the first item on the list that
Wise William had given them.

"Now we need to find an egg,"
said Jack.

"Let's go and visit Kind Kamila!"
said Sam.

18

"Hello, Kind Kamila,"
said Jack and Sam.

"What a lovely surprise to see you!"
replied Kind Kamila,
"What may I do for you?"

20

"We need your help. You see, we want to have our own twin kangaroos and we were wondering if you would let us have some of your eggs," they said.

"Oh, yes of course!" said Kind Kamila with a smile, "I have lots of them and would love to give you some, which means that I would be an egg donor and will help you have your own twin kangaroos."

Very early next morning,
Jack and Sam went to visit
Sweet Susan to ask her if she would
lend her pouch for a few months so
that their twin kangaroos
could grow inside her.

"Oh, yes of course!"
said Sweet Susan with a smile,
"I would love to lend you my pouch
for a few months, which means that
I would be a surrogate
for your twin baby kangaroo."

Jack and Sam were very excited that they had found everything listed on **The Twin Kangaroo Treasure Hunt** scroll and immediately went to visit Wise William again to see what they had to do next.

Wise William congratulated them for having completed the first part of the list so quickly.

"Now you need..." said Wise William, while Jack and Sam listened very carefully, "Now you need to go with Dr. Good Gotunda who knows how to bring together everything on **The Twin Kangaroo Treasure Hunt list**".

"Please promise to visit me when your twin kangaroos are born," he said enthusiastically.

In the clinic, Dr. Good Gotunda gently put
Kind Kamila's eggs and the sperms together in a
test tube and patiently looked after them until
they fertilized and formed two embryos.

When the embryos started to grow,
Dr. Good Gotunda placed them
into Sweet Susan's womb,
hidden in her pouch,
where they continued...

to grow...
and grow...
and grow!..

A few months later Sweet Susan gave birth to Jack and Sam's twin kangaroos.

At last, Jack and Sam
went to visit Wise William.

Now they were a very
happy family, with their twins.

Their much desired treasure.

CPSIA information can be obtained
at www.ICGtesting.com
Printed in the USA
LVIC060347110419
613621LV00025B/433

9 786070 065453